D0382278

SPOTLIGHT ON NATIVE AMERICANS

# BLACKFOOT

Chelly Dwyer

PowerKiDS
press.

New York

Published in 2016 by The Rosen Publishing Group, Inc.
29 East 21st Street, New York, NY 10010

First Edition

Editor: Karolena Bielecki
Book Design: Kris Everson
Reviewed by: Robert J. Conley, Former Sequoyah Distinguished Professor at Western Carolina University and Director of Native American Studies at Morningside College and Montana State University
Supplemental material reviewed by: Donald A. Grinde, Jr., Professor of Transnational/American Studies at the State University of New York at Buffalo.

Photo Credits: Cover © John E Marriott/All Canada Photos/age fotostock; pp. 4–5 © Salvatore Vasapolli/Animals Animals/age fotostock; pp. 7, 21 Peter Newark's American Pictures; p. 9 Mary Evans Picture Library; pp. 10–11 © Roy Ooms/All Canada Photos/age fotostock; pp. 13, 14, 25 Corbis; pp. 17, 24, 27 Native Stock; p. 19 (Buyenlarge) Getty Images; pp. 22–23 Wolfgang Kaehler/SuperStock; p. 29 © Michelle Gilders/age fotostock.

Library of Congress Cataloging-in-Publication Data

Dwyer, Chelly.
  Blackfoot / Chelly Dwyer.
      pages cm. — (Spotlight on Native Americans)
  Includes bibliographical references and index.
  ISBN 978-1-4994-1686-2 (pbk.)
  ISBN 978-1-4994-1685-5 (6 pack)
  ISBN 978-1-4994-1688-6 (library binding)
  1. Siksika Indians—Social life and customs—Juvenile literature. 2. Siksika Indians—History—Juvenile literature. I. Title.
  E99.S54D93 2016
  978.004'97352—dc23
                                        2015008151

Manufactured in the United States of America

# CONTENTS

# THE BLACKFOOT CONFEDERATION

## CHAPTER 1

The Blackfoot are a **confederation** of separate tribes. The Kainai (also called Blood) with 9,400 members, the Siksika (or Northern Blackfoot) with 4,200 members, and the Piikani (or Piegan) with 2,800 members all live in Canada. With 15,560 members, the Southern Piegan call themselves Blackfeet and live in the United States. These tribes share the Algonquian language and have very similar cultures. In the past, the white newcomers to North America thought these tribes were all the same. Today, the Blackfoot Confederacy is a political union of the different tribes that works with the U.S. and Canadian governments.

The Blackfoot people traditionally occupied an area east of the Rocky Mountains in Alberta, Saskatchewan, and Montana. Their territory stretched almost to the North Saskatchewan River in the north and the Missouri River in the south. Today, they live on the Blood, Piegan, and Blackfoot **Reserves** in Alberta, Canada, and the Blackfeet **Reservation** in Montana in the United States.

The Blackfoot people's name came from the neighboring Cree people, who called them siksikauw, or "black-footed people," because the bottoms of their moccasins were black. The Blackfoot people call themselves Niitsitapii, or "the real people."

Chief Mountain sits among the yellow leaves of aspen trees in autumn in the Blackfeet Reservation in Montana.

# HISTORY AND EARLY EUROPEAN CONTACT

### CHAPTER 2

The Blackfoot tribes originally lived in northeastern Canada and Maine and slowly moved southwest to the plains of Saskatchewan, Alberta, and Montana. They used dogs and travois (a simple sled made with two poles holding a platform for a load), following the buffalo as they moved from the open prairie in the summer and fall to the more sheltered forests in the winter.

Constantly at war over territory and access to the buffalo with neighboring tribes, the Blackfoot people were defeated in 1730 when, for the first time, the Shoshones rode horses into battle. The Blackfoot wanted horses and turned to their **allies**, probably the Flathead, Kootenai, or Nez Perce Indians, for help in getting them. The Cree Indians gave them another advantage—the rifle, which they had obtained from European traders.

By 1754, the Blackfoot were mounted on horses and knew about metal axes, knives, and other items the Europeans brought to exchange with other Native

To gather foods and hunt, the Blackfoot people often moved their camps. Tepees and household goods were packed onto a travois, which was originally pulled by a large dog and later a horse.

groups. Blackfoot tribes began trading in the 1780s, carrying dried meat, buffalo robes, and furs to British forts. Among the first European Americans the Blackfoot people saw were those from the Meriwether Lewis and William Clark expedition of 1804 to 1806.

# CONFLICTS AND TREATIES

## CHAPTER 3

After the discovery of gold in California in 1849, settlers poured west. In 1855, Isaac Stevens, the governor of the Northwest Territory, which included Blackfoot land, signed the Lame Bull **Treaty** with the tribe. The Blackfoot were promised a large reservation in Montana, annual payments, and training to be ranchers and farmers if they left settlers alone and allowed railroads and telegraphs to be built on their land.

Some Blackfoot people fought the invading settlers during the Blackfoot War of 1865 to 1870. The only U.S. military action against the Blackfoot tribe, the Marias River Massacre, occurred in 1870, when Major Eugene Baker attacked Blackfoot chief Heavy Runner's camp by mistake and killed about two hundred innocent people.

In 1870, the Hudson's Bay Company, which owned all of western Canada, sold the Blackfoot territory to the Canadian government. In 1877, the government signed Treaty 7 with the Blackfoot tribes living in Canada. The Blackfoot chiefs gave up 50,000 square miles (129,500 square kilometers) of hunting grounds in exchange for reserves, annual payments, and tools for farming and ranching. Most of the people continued their traditional hunting lifestyles until the buffalo herds were nearly wiped out by American hide hunters.

Miners like these wanted to look for copper and gold in the Montana mountains and pressured the U.S. government to buy more than 1 million acres (405,000 ha) from the Blackfoot people and move the native residents out. Nothing of mineral value was found; the area later became Glacier National Park.

# LIFE ON RESERVATIONS
## CHAPTER 4

After the disappearance of the buffalo, around 1879, the Blackfoot people had no choice but to move to their government-assigned lands and try to make a living in a different way. Poorly prepared to make this change, many people died during the Starvation Winter of 1883 to 1884.

In Montana, the Southern Piegans moved onto their reservation and became known as the Blackfeet. Beginning in 1907, the U.S. government forced them to divide the reservation land into individual parcels and opened the rest of their land to white settlers. This

division continued until the Indian Reorganization Act of 1934. The tribe adopted a **constitution** and formed a council to oversee their reservation lands in 1935.

The Piikani, Kainai, and Siksika all moved onto their Canadian reserves and were pressured to give up their lands as well. Only the Kainai were able to keep their reserve from shrinking; it remains the largest reserve in Canada.

All the tribes became dependent upon government food **rations** and tried to become ranchers and farmers, building log cabins to live in. Christian **missionaries** started **boarding schools** and took the children away from their homes to educate them, usually forcing them to abandon their Native culture.

The Blackfoot people had relied heavily on the buffalo. The buffalo population declined after being over-hunted.

# THE BLACKFOOT IN THE TWENTIETH CENTURY

## CHAPTER 5

During World War II (1939–1945), many men moved off the Blackfeet Reservation and joined the U.S. military, where they learned new skills. The remaining Blackfeet ranched and raised farm animals on their lands. A 1964 flood resulted in emergency money being given to the reservation to build houses, roads, and dams.

After the war, the Canadian government began to improve social services on the reserves, where most of the Canadian Blackfoot people remained, and began a strong agricultural program. By the 1970s, modern housing and electricity were introduced to the Canadian Blackfoot reserves.

In the 1950s, alcohol sales were allowed on U.S. Blackfeet land and in the 1960s on Canadian reserves, encouraging **alcoholism** and creating many health and social problems. By the 1960s, many Blackfoot children on both sides of the border attended **integrated** schools and went on to college, returning to the reservation or reserves to work as managers, welfare officers, teachers, and nurses. In 1976, Red Crow College opened on the Blood Reserve and Blackfeet Community College on the Blackfeet Reservation. Much of the reservation and reserve social life revolves around sports such as rodeo, hockey, and basketball.

World War II was the first time that many Blackfeet people left the reservation. Here at Camp Lejeune, North Carolina, Marine Corps reservists Minnie Spotted Wolf (Blackfeet), Celia Mix (Potawatomi), and Viola Eastman (Ojibwe) pose in their uniforms in 1943.

# NOMADIC TRADITIONS
## CHAPTER 6

The Blackfoot bands were **nomadic**, and they moved often. They spent the longest time in their winter camp, beginning in late October or early November. Each band wintered separately, erecting tepees in river valley woods. They wore fur clothes for warmth. If no

When many Blackfoot bands gathered to camp together in the summer, each band, and each family in the band, had a certain spot where they always put their tepee.

fresh game was found, they ate dried meat, roots, and **pemmican**.

In spring, the men hunted small animals until the band caught up with the buffalo. Spring was the time to gather new tepee poles, make clothing for the warm weather, and repair riding equipment.

In June, the bands gathered for the annual tribal buffalo hunt. The hunt provided lots of fresh meat, new buffalo hides for tepees and clothing, and buffalo tongues for the Sun Dance. The annual Sun Dance ceremony began in August. A time for feasting, wearing fancy clothes, and meeting friends, it also provided an opportunity for dancing and singing for the good of the tribe.

Then, the bands moved as much as necessary to stay with the buffalo. Women gathered berries and dried the buffalo meat for pemmican. If there was extra food and buffalo robes, the band would visit a trading post. As the weather worsened, the band moved into its winter camp.

# SOCIAL STRUCTURE
## CHAPTER 7

The Blackfoot bands were small, extended family groups with no formal organization other than a recognized leader. If a band became too large, the people would split into two smaller bands. Bands used names based upon some event or the people in them, such as Many Fat Horses band and All Short People band.

Leaders were men who were brave warriors and generous to the poor. They worked hard to keep order by ending arguments and making final decisions for all of the people.

Men hunted animals for food, cared for their horses, and protected their band and its territory. They were away from camp a lot, hunting and leading raids, while women's lives were based in camp. Women prepared food, raised children, and cared for the sacred bundles, which were groups of objects tied in a cloth or hide package that they used for religious ceremonies. Because the women

Upon the death of a Blackfoot chief, certain personal belongings were kept with his body, and the rest of his wealth was distributed to the tribe according to his wishes. These people are dividing up the wealth of a chief who died around 1901.

owned the tepees and everything inside them, they were responsible for preparing dried foods such as pemmican, **tanning** hides, and sewing and decorating clothes and tepees.

# FAMILY LIFE

## CHAPTER 8

When a child was about to be born, the mother left camp and was cared for by a **medicine woman**. After birth, the baby was washed, prayed over, and painted red. The baby's **umbilical cord** was cut with an arrowhead and then dried and preserved in a beaded container: a snake shape for a boy's and a lizard shape for a girl's. Blackfoot people believed that snakes and lizards were never sick and lived long lives, and they wished this for their children. A few days after birth, the father asked a relative or important person to officially name the baby. This name was a girl's forever, but a boy could earn many names.

Boys and girls played together until they were about five years old, then mothers began to teach the girls their responsibilities. The girls started by gathering wood, picking berries, and digging roots, soon learning how to prepare food, tan hides, and put up and take down a tepee. Fathers trained their sons to shoot with bows and

Young Blackfoot women collecting goldenrod around 1910. Goldenrod is one of the medicinal plants used frequently by Native Americans. This is one of the plants that Old Man, the mythical creator of the world, would have shown to the Blackfoot people.

arrows, guard horses, and follow animal tracks. When a boy killed his first animal or a girl finished her first beadwork, the family held a feast to celebrate.

# BELIEFS AND CEREMONIES

## CHAPTER 9

The most important Blackfoot god was Sun; his wife was Moon, and Morning Star was their child. Many animals and birds also possessed **supernatural** powers. Old Man, or Napi, was not only the creator of the world but a trickster. Old Man stories were told to teach children lessons.

Most ceremonies were based on medicine bundles, which were sacred. Each one was different. Usually, a young man would go away from the camp and stay out for several nights. He **fasted** and called upon the gods and spirits. They would come to him in a dream, give him a power, and show him the items that should be in his sacred medicine bundle. Then it was up to him to gather the objects. Sometimes the man would also be shown designs to paint on his tepee.

The Blackfoot people adopted the Sun Dance from other Plains tribes, probably in the early 1800s. Their most important ceremony was called the Medicine Lodge. A respected woman always planned and paid for this ceremony. This involved buying the medicine bundle

This Blackfoot warrior is participating in the Sun Dance by tying himself to a center pole with strips of leather that are pierced through his skin. He will dance until his skin tears and he pulls free, showing his bravery and dedication to his community.

from the previous sponsor of the Medicine Lodge, supplying hundreds of buffalo tongues, and building a lodge using one hundred willows.

# THE BLACKFOOT TODAY
## CHAPTER 10

Educational and employment opportunities continue to improve for the Blackfoot people, but they are still dealing with the social problems created by alcohol beginning in the 1950s and 1960s. Reserves and reservations offer social services for alcoholism, **addiction**, family problems, and unemployment.

The Kainai (Blood) reserve is the largest in Canada and supports a farming operation that grows grain and other crops. The Piikani (Piegan) reserve owns a successful clothing factory and sells arts and crafts. The elders help at Head-Smashed-In National Monument, explaining their traditional way of life to tourists. The Siksika (Northern Blackfoot) reserve, containing 175,400 acres (71,000 ha) of land, arranged self-government with Canada in 2010.

In the United States, the Blackfeet Reservation, on 1.5 million acres (607,300 ha) in northwest Montana, relies on tourism dollars. The reservation is located next to Glacier National Park. It has also opened a **casino** and it **leases** land to oil and natural gas companies. Beef cattle farming is another source of income.

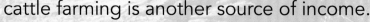

All of the Blackfoot nations have an elected council of leaders that makes decisions for the tribe. The three Canadian tribes belong to an organization of Treaty 7 tribes as well as the national First Nations Council.

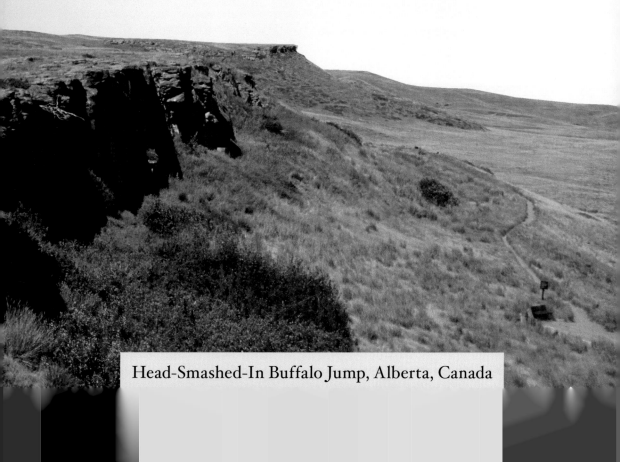

Head-Smashed-In Buffalo Jump, Alberta, Canada

# PRESERVING BLACKFOOT CULTURE

## CHAPTER 11

All of the Blackfoot tribes are concerned with maintaining their unique language and culture while improving and increasing the jobs available on their reserves. By taking control of the schools that their children attend, they feel they can again take part in their education and share the traditional Blackfoot values. The Blackfoot language is taught in preschool, elementary school, and high

Because of increased opportunities on the reservation and reserves, these Blackfeet girls growing up today have an opportunity to learn the Blackfoot language and go to college.

school programs on the reserves. The Red Crow College in Alberta, Canada, with a new Kainai Studies degree program, and the Blackfeet Community College in Montana are both tribal colleges.

Teachers at the immersion school in Browning, Montana, speak and write only in the Blackfoot language to help the young children in their classes become fluent in their traditional language.

On the Blackfeet reservation, the Piegan Institute has promoted the Blackfoot language since 1987. It runs an immersion school in Browning, Montana, where children from kindergarten to grade 8 are taught in their native language, and no English is spoken. The Piegan Institute also produces written, audio, and video information on Blackfoot language and history.

The Canadian reserves have focused on tribal independence. These tribes have slowly taken control of the health, social, economic, and educational services on their reserves so that they can include tribal language and traditions in the schools and other services.

# BLACKFOOT LITERATURE AND ART

## CHAPTER 12

Beverly Hungry Wolf has written several books about the Blackfoot people, including two that focus on Blackfoot women. *The Ways of My Grandmothers* (1980) features stories about women collected from respected older Blackfoot women in Canada. *Daughters of the Buffalo Women: Maintaining the Tribal Faith* (1996) is a collection of memories of older women who grew up in the early 1900s on reservations and in boarding schools.

Harold Gray (Long Standing Bear Chief), who died in 2010, also wrote about the Native American way of life, producing many books and articles for both adults and children.

The Blackfoot people have always been known for their moccasins. Left plain for daily wear, moccasins were decorated with fancy beading for special occasions. Because Blackfoot women used stiff porcupine quills to decorate moccasins, early designs were **geometrical**. When beads became available at trading posts, they began to design curved patterns. Using solid white or blue

Colorful beadwork decorates this traditional Blackfoot hide dress, worn at a contemporary powwow.

beads for the background, Blackfoot women created new flower designs as well as following traditional patterns. Today's Blackfoot artists sometimes bead moccasins using the very old traditional designs, but they often borrow designs from other Native American tribes or use the popular Blackfoot flower designs in their beadwork.

# A STRONG CONFEDERACY

## CHAPTER 13

In 1998, all four of the Blackfoot tribes began a movement to reestablish the Blackfoot Confederacy, made up of the Siksika, Piikani, and Kainai tribes from Canada and the U.S. Blackfeet. The Blackfoot Confederacy works with museums to return tribal treasures, addresses border difficulties, and brings jobs and government funding to the tribes.

The U.S.–Canadian border can sometimes cause problems for members. On one occasion, Canadian Kainai Chief Chris Shade couldn't bring his eagle-feather headdress into the United States. In the United States, Native Americans must have a permit to have eagle feathers since eagles are a protected species by law. Because Canada doesn't have the same law, Chief Shade had no permit, and his headdress had to stay in Canada.

In 2009, the Blackfeet Tribal Business Council created Chief Mountain Technologies, based in Browning, Montana, to create tech jobs for tribal members. Members are also now benefiting from money paid to the nation by oil companies that are looking for new sources of oil.

The Blackfoot people are moving forward, solving their own problems, and maintaining the important traditions that make them who they are.

This Blackfoot man is dancing at a powwow in Alberta, Canada, to commemorate the signing of Treaty 7, a treaty between the Blackfoot people and the Canadian government.

# GLOSSARY

**addiction:** The condition of being dependent on a substance, thing, or activity.

**alcoholism:** A disease in which people's desire to drink alcohol is so strong they cannot control it.

**ally:** One of two or more people or groups who work together.

**boarding school:** A school where students must live on school grounds.

**casino:** A building where gambling takes place.

**confederation:** A group of people or nations joined together for a common purpose.

**constitution:** The basic laws and principles of a nation that outline the powers of the government and the rights of the people.

**fast:** To go without eating.

**geometrical:** Describing a design with regular lines and shapes.

**integrated:** Made up of a mixed group of people.

**lease:** To allow someone to use land or property for a specified amount of time in return for money.

**medicine woman:** A religious leader and healer.

**missionary:** Someone who tries to teach others their religion.

**nomadic:** Not having a single home but moving from place to place in search of food or following groups of animals.

**pemmican:** Dried meat that's pounded into a powder and mixed with animal fat and dried berries.

**ration:** Food allowances given out a little at a time.

**reservation:** Land set aside by the U.S. government for a specific Native American tribe to live on.

**reserve:** Land set aside by the Canadian government for a specific Native American tribe to live on.

**supernatural:** Describing something believed to be beyond scientific explanation and the laws of nature.

**tanning:** Changing animal hide into leather by soaking it in liquid containing acid.

**treaty:** An agreement among nations or people.

**umbilical cord:** A flexible structure that connects a baby to its mother in the womb.

# FOR MORE INFORMATION

## BOOKS

King, David C. *The Blackfeet*. New York, NY: Marshall
    Cavendish, 2010.
Lacey, Theresa Jensen. *The Blackfeet*. New York, NY:
    Chelsea House, 2011.
Tieck, Sarah. *Blackfoot*. Edina, MN: ABDO Publishing
    Company, 2015.

## WEBSITES

Due to the changing nature of Internet links, PowerKids Press has developed an online list of websites related to the subject of this book. This site is updated regularly. Please use this link to access the list: www.powerkidslinks.com/sona/foot

# INDEX